FABULOUS FONDUES

FABULOUS FONDUES

By Dorothy H. Becker

and

Nancy S. Wallace

———

Illustrations by Maggie Jarvis

PETER PAUPER PRESS
Mount Vernon, New York

FONDUE

F-rugal

O-pportunity for hostess to relax

N-utritious

D-unking is friendly

U-niversal

E-asy to prepare

FABULOUS FONDUES

FOR PARTIES IN A POT

Fondue is the Cinderella of the food world. Once upon a time this simple peasant dish was the main meal for the family. Cooked and served in the same pot, it was placed in the center of the table. The family gathered round and dunked their bread in the bubbling caquelon.

Green summer pastures and fall harvests provided the basis for an abundance of bread and cheese which became the staple diet. Naturally the longer the cheese and bread aged, the harder it became. Since the winters were long, it became very hard. Sometimes the bread was so hard, it was actually cut with an axe!

One day a farmer's wife dropped a piece of cheese on the hearth and it melted. Being a creative cook, she thought of dipping her hardened bread into the oozing cheese. Thus, a simple, delicious meal was originated.

Today, from these simple beginnings, this ancient dish has evolved to a party in a pot, enjoyed by all, from teen-agers to senior citizens. Fondue is indeed a fairy tale princess in today's food world!

POTS AND PANS

It would be hard to improve on the farmer's heavy earthenware pot or caquelon. Yet any flameproof, earthenware or cast-iron casserole will do the job, as long as it is round and holds the heat. Since the fondue can be started on the kitchen stove, be sure that the casserole can withstand the direct heat of the fire.

A metal fondue cooker is best for Fondue Bourguignonne or other meat fondues because metal conducts the heat more rapidly, allowing your meat to cook quickly. Select from a vast array of metal fondue cookers in your neighborhood store — copper, stainless steel, or vari-colored enamelware, with tray to match.

A warmer is necessary to keep the fondue bubbling on the table. Use an electric hot plate, warming tray or alcohol flame. Fuel is available either in the canned form or as liquid used with a wick. A heavy chafing dish can also be used.

Long fondue forks, preferably with a wooden handle, are best for spearing the bread or meat, but metal skewers, hibachi sticks, chopsticks or metal knitting needles will also do nicely.

FONDUE FUELS

The fuel you use will vary according to the heat source designed for the pot you've bought.

Some are just candles. These are "warmers" only and are more satisfactory for the dessert fondues.

Then there's canned heat, a semi-solid available in small tins with tightly fitting lids.

Most lamp types use denatured alcohol, a liquid available at drug, hardware and department stores.

One of the newest innovations in fondue cooking is the electric fondue pot, available in decorator colors. It is an ensemble of a teflon lined pot and an electrical tray type unit. Easy to clean, it gives an even source of heat without danger of flame when hot oil is used as in the beef fondue.

An electric skillet can be used but the deep and rounded utensils are more suitable for fondue cookery.

WHICH CHEESE?

The original and best Swiss cheese, famous for its holes and imitated all over the world, is the Switzerland Emmenthaler. Made in large wheels, it is traditionally marked in bright red with the country of origin. Another well-liked cheese from Switzerland with smaller holes and a stronger flavor, is Gruyère.

Both cheeses melt well and are the basis for the classic fondue. Proportions of each cheese used are a matter of personal taste. However, the more Gruyère used the less salt needed as Gruyère is more heavily salted.

Emmenthaler and Gruyère are preferred because they are well matured. American Swiss and many other cheeses which melt well are not as well matured but will give very good results. Even though you select the cheese with care, your cooking technique is equally important.

COOKING WITH CHEESE

Cheese is perhaps the oldest of the convenience foods. It is a highly concentrated source of protein without waste, has a minimum amount of spoilage and it is almost one hundred percent digestible.

The important thing about cooking with cheese is not to overcook it. If the heat is too high or the cooking is prolonged, the cheese will become tough and stringy.

SPECIAL COOKING TIPS

A third-pound of cheese is a reasonable amount to allow for each guest, although it varies with your guests' appetites.

One-third cup of wine is the correct proportion for each third-pound of cheese.

Four ounces of cheese equals one standard measuring cup of grated cheese.

Dice the cheese so that it will melt more quickly.

Grated cheese tends to form lumps when cooking.

If in a rush, don't grate! Shred the cheese.

Dredge the cheese with flour for smooth consistency.

Avoid a tough fondue by cooking no more than one pound of cheese at a time.

Keep the cheese hot and bubbling, stirring constantly.

WHERE TO KEEP CHEESE

As a rule all cheeses will keep for several weeks when well-wrapped and kept on the top shelf just below the freezer. Many refrigerator doors have a special butter or cheese storage compartment.

To wrap cheese for storage, soak a cloth in a mild brine solution, wring it out well and wrap the cheese tightly. Wrap again in plastic wrap or aluminum foil. This will cut down on the formation of mold and keep the cheese from drying out.

MILD BRINE

½ teaspoon salt
½ cup water
1 tablespoon dry wine or lemon juice

Dry wine improves the cheese flavor.

Should your cheese develop a slight mold on the outside, just cut off the mold and the inner cheese is as good as fresh-bought.

Leftover bits of cheese can be grated and kept in a tightly covered jar in the refrigerator or made into a savory canapé spread.

SWISS SPREAD

½ cup butter
2 ounces grated Swiss cheese
Brandy to moisten

Mix all ingredients to a creamy consistency. To keep indefinitely, store in a small crock in the refrigerator. Remove from the refrigerator about one hour before serving.

Any cheese tastes more flavorful at room temperature.

WINES

Cheese is to milk as wine is to grapes.

Wine, like cheese, has countless varieties because of the variations in water, climate, and soil. No two wines can be identical if they are made in different locations. Naturally wine and cheese from the same geographic location seem to have a greater affinity of flavor. Yet wines and cheeses from distant localities may combine well together if they were grown in similar climates.

The light white wines call for delicately flavored Emmenthaler and Gruyère cheese.

Kirsch, a cherry-flavored brandy is tradtionally used with these cheeses in fondues.

Chablis is a good substitute for the more expensive brandy and can be used in combination with the Kirsch.

The acidity of the wine helps to melt the cheese and make a smoother fondue. If the wine is not sufficiently acid, add a little lemon juice — about one teaspoon lemon juice for each ⅓ cup of wine.

TYPICAL CHEESE FONDUE MENU

CLASSIC CHEESE FONDUE

FRENCH BREAD   BOWL OF RED APPLES

HOT MULLED CIDER

MERINGUE SHELLS WITH LIME SHERBET

CLASSIC FONDUE

2 loaves French or Italian bread
1 pound Emmenthaler cheese, diced
2 tablespoons flour
1 clove fresh garlic
2 cups dry white wine
1 tablespoon lemon juice
¼ cup Kirsch
Nutmeg and pepper or paprika to taste

1. Cut bread into 1″ squares with crust on one side of each square.
2. Place cheese in a bowl and sprinkle with flour. Mix so that each piece is coated with flour.
3. Rub casserole and wooden stirring spoon with cut clove of garlic.
4. Pour wine into casserole and place over moderate heat until small bubbles rise to the top (simmering; not boiling). Add lemon juice.

5. Add cheese one handful at a time, stirring constantly until each handful is melted before adding another. Continue stirring until mixture starts to bubble lightly.
6. Add Kirsch and spices. Stir until well blended.
7. Put on table over warmer.

Serves four.

SERVING THE FONDUE

Spear a cube of bread with a long handled fondue fork. Push prongs through the soft part of the bread and then into the crust. This will prevent the bread from falling off the fork into the fondue pot. Swirl the fork in the fondue making a figure eight. This motion helps keep the fondue at the proper consistency as it coats the bread. Should the fondue thicken too rapidly, it can be readily thinned by returning to the stove and adding a small quantity of the slightly warmed (*not cold*) wine.

FORFEITS

Lose your bread cube in the fondue and you must pay a forfeit.

If you are a man, you pay for the next bottle of wine.

If you're a girl, you must kiss the man of your choice.

THE PRIZE POT

As the fondue disappears, a thin brown crust of melted cheese forms at the bottom of the casserole. Remove from heat and share this delicacy among those who have not lost a bread cube.

VARIATIONS OF CLASSIC CHEESE FONDUE

Use the same classic recipe exactly as given with these variations:

Use ½ lb. Emmenthaler and ½ lb. Gruyère cheese.

Use ⅓ lb. Emmenthaler, ⅓ lb. Gruyère and ⅓ lb. Tilsiter cheese.

Use ½ lb. Emmenthaler and ½ lb. caraway cheese. (Leyden is an excellent caraway cheese!)

Use 1 lb. Gruyère cheese.

Use ⅓ lb. Gorgonzola, ⅓ lb. Tilsiter, and ⅓ lb. Gruyère cheese.

OTHER TYPES OF VARIATIONS FOR CLASSIC FONDUE

HAM FONDUE

Sauté 2 cups diced cooked ham in butter. Add to the fondue before serving. Or you may spear the ham instead of bread and dunk in the fondue.

TRUFFLES FONDUE

Sauté drained chopped truffles in butter. Add to fondue about three minutes before serving. Heat thoroughly.

TOMATO FONDUE

Sauté 1 medium sliced onion in 3 tablespoons melted butter until translucent. Remove onion and reserve. Add 3 peeled, seeded and quartered fresh tomatoes to the remaining butter. Cook over low fire until tomatoes have a "melted" look . . . approximately 30 minutes. Add onions and blend. Add ½ teaspoon basil and a pinch of sugar. Combine with fondue just long enough before serving for mixture to become thoroughly hot.

ATTENTION! CREATIVE COOKS!

ADDITIONAL ALTERNATIVES FOR CHEESE FONDUE

Substitute for Kirsch:

Dry Rum   Brandy
Slivovitz   Apple Jack

Suitable Wines:

Vermouth   Neuchatel
Chablis   Reisling
Dry Champagne

Other Seasonings:

Scallions   Cayenne
Horseradish   Catsup
Parsley   Tomato Juice
Thyme   Mayonnaise
Mustard

Other Cheeses:

Caperhilly   Parmesan
Cheshire   Fontina
Canadian Cheddar

Other Flavors:

Lobster   Chicken
Crabmeat   Salmon

Possible Vegetable Seasonings:

Spinach   Avocado
Asparagus

ADDITIONAL ALTERNATIVES FOR FRENCH OR ITALIAN BREAD

Boiled potatoes (small or cubed).

Potato chips (warmed in oven).

Crackers.

Butter fried croutons.

Bread sticks.

Celery sticks.

Pretzels.

Lightly toasted bread cubes or fingers.

Corn chips.

Rusks.

Rye Bread.

Toasted Brioche.

Melba Toast.

Hard Rolls.

Soup Nuts.

MUSHROOM FONDUE

2 loaves French bread
1 pound Swiss cheese, diced
2 tablespoons flour
1 clove garlic
2 cups dry sherry
1 tablespoon lemon juice
¼ cup fresh mushrooms, minced
1 tablespoon minced onion
1 tablespoon butter
2 tablespoons Kirsch
Nutmeg and pepper to taste

1. Cut bread into 1″ squares with crust on one side of each square.

2. Place cheese in bowl and sprinkle with flour. Mix well so that cheese is coated with flour.

3. Rub casserole and wooden stirring spoon with cut clove of garlic.

4. Sauté mushrooms and onion in butter in skillet until golden — about three minutes.

5. Pour wine into casserole and place over moderate heat until small bubbles rise to the top (simmering, not boiling). Add lemon juice, onions and mushrooms.

6. Add cheese one handful at a time, stirring constantly until each handful is melted before adding another. Continue stirring until mixture starts to bubble lightly.

7. Add Kirsch and spices. Stir until well blended.

8. Put on table over warmer.

Serves four.

FONDUE FINES HERBES

2 loaves French or Italian bread
1 pound Swiss cheese, diced
2 tablespoons flour
1 clove fresh garlic
2 cups Chablis
1 egg yolk
½ teaspoon Fines Herbes
Freshly ground pepper

1. Cut bread into 1″ squares with crust on one side of each square.

2. Place cheese in a bowl and sprinkle with flour. Mix so that each piece is coated with flour.

3. Rub casserole and wooden stirring spoon with cut clove of garlic.

4. Pour wine into casserole and place over moderate heat until small bubbles rise to the top (simmering, but not boiling).

5. Add cheese one handful at a time, stirring constantly until each handful is melted before adding another. Continue stirring until mixture starts to bubble lightly.

6. Stir a small amount of hot cheese mixture into beaten egg yolk. Then add egg to hot cheese. This method prevents coagulation of the egg and a curdled appearance.

7. Add Fines Herbes and pepper to taste.

NOTE: Fines Herbes are a mixture of thyme, oregano, sage, rosemary, marjoram and basil.

TUNA FONDUE

8 to 10 slices toasted bread
7 oz. tuna, drained (one can)
1 can condensed celery soup
½ cup cream
1 cup shredded American cheese
2 tablespoons flour
2 teaspoons onion juice

¼ cup finely chopped green pepper
¼ cup finely chopped pimento
1 teaspoon celery salt
¼ teaspoon white pepper
½ cup sauterne

1. Cut toasted bread in 1″ squares.

2. Drain oil from tuna. Rinse under running warm water in a strainer. Flake tuna with a fork until very finely separated. Reserve.

3. Mix can of condensed celery soup with ½ cup cream until smooth. Cook over low heat.

4. Sprinkle shredded cheese with flour. Reserve.

5. Add onion juice, green pepper, pimento, celery salt and pepper to the soup mixture and mix well. Continue to cook over low heat.

6. Add wine slowly to soup mixture stirring constantly until bubbling hot.

7. Add a handful of cheese at a time. Stir constantly over low flame until cheese is melted.

8. Blend in tuna and heat thoroughly.

9. Taste and add salt (or garlic salt) if desired. Keep hot for dunking bread squares.

CHIVE FONDUE

Basket of cubed bread
½ lb. Swiss cheese, diced
½ lb. Appenzeller cheese, diced
4 tablespoons flour
1 cut clove of garlic
2 tablespoons butter
4 tablespoons chives, fresh or frozen
1¼ cups dry sherry
½ teaspoon Worcestershire sauce
Pinch of nutmeg
Pinch of paprika
¼ teaspoon white pepper
3 tablespoons apple jack
Salt to taste

1. Mix cheese and flour. Reserve.

2. Rub pot with cut clove of garlic.

3. Melt butter in pot and cook chives in butter for about thirty seconds. Keep heat very low.

4. Add sherry. When just simmering begin adding cheese a handful at a time. Stir after each addition of cheese until just melted.

5. Continue to stir constantly over low heat and add Worcestershire, nutmeg, paprika, pepper and apple jack.

6. Add salt to taste.

7. Keep hot while dunking bread.

Serves 4.

TEETOTALERS' FONDUE

1 lb. Swiss cheese, diced
Cold milk to cover cheese
3 tablespoons butter
6 egg yolks
¼ teaspoon white pepper
Basket of bread cubes

1. Soak diced cheese in milk at least 8 hours.

2. Melt butter in flameproof casserole. Stir with a wooden spoon.

3. Add cheese gradually after draining. Reserve drained milk. Continue stirring butter and cheese over low heat.

4. Beat egg yolks until foamy. Add small amount of the hot mixture to the egg yolks; then stir egg mixture into remaining hot mixture. Cook and stir over low heat until smooth.

30

5. Add pepper and enough of the re-
   served milk after it is heated to keep
   the mixture at a smooth dunkable consistency. Add milk in small splashes.
   About half the milk will probably be
   needed.

6. Keep hot for dunking.

Serves 4.

This is a non-alcoholic fondue. However
you need not have fears about using wines
as the heat evaporates the volatile spirits
leaving only the wine flavoring.

BEEF FONDUE

Fondue Bourguignonne, another famous
Swiss dish, is not technically a fondue because it has no melted cheese; and it is
not made with Burgundy wine as most
people think its name suggests.

Instead it is a cheeseless, wineless dish
that's fun to serve. It's an informal way
for your guests to spear their bite-size
meat on long wooden-handled forks, cook
right at the table in bubbling hot oil and
dip into their well-seasoned sauce or ac-
companiment.

As with a cheese fondue, beef fondue is an evening's entertainment.

Invite only four to six friends unless you have more than one fondue pot. Too many cooking at one time isn't feasible because of the pot's narrow opening and because the oil cools too quickly.

It's easy on the hostess who has only to buy the food as her guests do the cooking to their own individual taste.

It's almost a spontaneous meal. Just one half hour from refrigerator to table—even less if your meat is already cubed.

No need to plan special table decorations as the fondue pot and the accompaniments are sufficiently colorful. Since it's a very casual gathering, it is not the place for the best table linens.

It's a good icebreaker as each person becomes an instant chef. Particularly the men. For what man doesn't think he knows best how rare a steak should be, and how to mix a sauce?

It's the ideal meal for late comers and long stayers.

A perfect way for beginners to entertain!

POTS AND PLATES

A metal fondue pot is best for Fondue Bourguignonne. Choose the metal to fit your decor. Copper is charming and cozy, reflecting warm firelight. Stainless steel suggests modern sophistication. Vari-colored enamel is gay and informal. The shape of all remains basically the same.

The specially inward curving sides result in a small opening which protects against excessive heat loss and reduces the chance for spattering oil.

Specially designed plates will give your party an added fillip. They are the size of a salad plate with individual sections for the meat and sauces. Lacking these you can use regular plates, although the sauces tend to run together.

Each guest should have two forks. The one for cooking the meat will get hot. The second is for dipping the cooked meat into sauces and eating. Should you have more guests than long handled forks, see that each guest has one fondue fork to cook the meat and one dinner fork with which to eat.

Use an extra large napkin.

COOKING WITH OIL

Choosing the oil to use is difficult. Ask any cook and you will find each opinion varies as to which will give the best result. There's olive, coconut, peanut, safflower, corn and other vegetable oils. There's butter and hydrogenated shortening to melt down.

Each has its advantages and you select your favorite oil or combination. Bear in mind that coconut oil doesn't foam or leave an after taste; butter must be clarified to prevent burning. Any good commercial oil that doesn't take on a strong flavor or smoke when boiled can be used.

TO CLARIFY BUTTER

Melt one cup (½ pound or 2 sticks) of butter in the top of a double boiler over boiling water. A white sediment will settle to the bottom of the pan. These milk solids which burn so readily when butter is used for sautéing also give a bitter taste to the food.

Strain through a loosely woven cloth to remove the sediment. You now have clarified butter which will keep about three weeks in a tightly covered jar in the refrigerator.

This can be used for all your sautéing. Save the sediment part for flavoring your vegetables in place of whole butter.

WHICH MEAT?

The cooking method used in preparing beef fondue demands the tenderest beef you can possibly select. Try explaining to the butcher how you plan to use his meat and he will undoubtedly be concerned that his reputation might suffer if he provides less than the best.

Buy five to seven ounces of the very finest quality beef tenderloin for each person. This is the only big expense you will have. If your budget simply won't cooperate, choose a sirloin or porterhouse. Unless the meat is one of these three cuts chances are you will need to use a tenderizer. But do use the tenderizer before you cube the meat. The rest of the meal is not only inexpensive but can probably be made from foods already on hand.

Have your butcher cut the beef in ¾ inch cubes, removing the fat. If you do it yourself, do it early in the day of the party or the night before. Store in a covered container in the refrigerator.

Take it out of the refrigerator and let stand about one hour until the beef reaches room temperature. This will prevent your oil from cooling off too quickly when cooking the meat, as each cube should cook thoroughly in only a few minutes.

SERVING

First bring out the tray and *unlighted* burner for the center of the table. Then the fondue pot which has been half filled with bubbling hot oil. *For safety's sake don't try to carry both at once.*

Light the burner at the same time you light the candles. The flickering lights add to the festive occasion. Our Swiss friends say you shouldn't start the party until dusk for the proper effect.

Fondue plates can be readied in the kitchen. Arrange beef cubes and well-seasoned sauces in an attractive manner. This is when the fondue plates are most helpful.

Or bring the beef to the table on a large platter or in a bowl. Use a bit of fresh green garnish on the uncooked meat. And put all the go-withs in those small bowls that are always in the back of the china closet.

Use them to make an attractive arrangement around the fondue pot.

For added drama, toss the green salad while at the table.

TYPICAL BEEF FONDUE MENU

BEEF BOURGUIGNONNE

BÉARNAISE SAUCE   CUMBERLAND SAUCE

CHUTNEY

CURRY CREAM   MUSTARD SAUCE

HORSERADISH CREAM

EGG SAUCE   SAUTÉED MUSHROOMS

TOSSED GREEN SALAD

OIL AND VINEGAR DRESSING

FRENCH BREAD   BUTTER

FRESH FRUIT CHAMPAGNE COMPOTE

COFFEE OR TEA

FONDUE BOURGUIGNONNE

2 pounds beef tenderloin, trimmed,
  cut into ¾ inch cubes
Cooking oil — enough to fill the
  fondue pot ½ full

Heat the cooking oil to 400° on the kitchen stove. Be sure it does not smoke. Put on the table over burner and let your guests spear a beef cube with the fondue fork and hold it in the hot oil until it is cooked to their liking.

Remember metal gets hot in the cooking oil, so it is necessary to transfer the meat to a cool fork. Dip into the sauce and eat!

Now you are ready to start the second beef cube cooking as the first fork has cooled.

Servings — approximately 6.

BÉARNAISE SAUCE

⅓ cup tarragon vinegar
¼ cup wine
1½ tablespoons finely chopped shallots
  (or green onions)
1 tablespoon finely minced parsley
¼ teaspoon salt
3 crushed peppercorns

½ teaspoon dried tarragon
3 egg yolks
1 cup butter
Dash cayenne pepper

1. Combine vinegar, wine, shallots, parsley, salt, crushed pepper and tarragon in a small saucepan. Bring to a boil and continue cooking until reduced to a thick paste. Cool.

2. Beat egg yolks in top of double boiler. Stir in vinegar mixture. Place *over* hot water (not boiling). Cook slowly, adding butter about 1 tablespoon at a time. Beat constantly with a whisk or fork. When thickened, stir in cayenne.

3. Serve cold.

Note: One secret is to not let the boiling water touch the bottom of the upper double boiler pan. In order to obtain the necessary smoothy textured sauce, you must cook slowly over low heat and add the butter as directed.

If in spite of your best efforts, you have bad luck and the sauce curdles, an emergency remedy is to add 1 to 2 tablespoons of boiling water and beat immediately and rapidly.

CUMBERLAND SAUCE

1 cup currant jelly
¼ cup port wine
Pulp of one medium orange
Pulp of ½ lemon
Pinch of ginger
Dash of cayenne

1. Melt currant jelly.

2. Add wine and crushed fruit pulp. Mix well.

3. Stir in spices.

4. Let stand for at least two hours so that flavors blend.

5. Serve at room temperature.

HORSERADISH CREAM

1 cup whipped cream
2 to 3 tablespoons horseradish
Salt to taste

1. Fold drained prepared horseradish into whipped cream.

2. Add salt to taste.

3. Serve cold.

CURRY CREAM

⅔ cup sour cream (or yoghurt)
⅓ cup mayonnaise
½ teaspoon grated lemon rind
Lemon juice to taste
Curry powder to taste

1. Mix sour cream or yoghurt and mayonnaise together.
2. Add other ingredients. The lemon juice and curry powder are added slowly bit by bit until it tastes good!
3. Serve cold.

MUSTARD SAUCE

2 tablespoons butter
1 tablespoon flour
2 cups chicken bouillon
1 tablespoon dry mustard
Salt and pepper to taste
¼ teaspoon lemon juice
2 egg yolks
3 tablespoons cream

Melt 1 tablespoon of butter. Stir in flour to make a paste. Stir in bouillon and cook over low heat (about 4 minutes) or until it begins to bubble and is slightly thickened. Add mustard, salt, pepper and lemon juice. Mix well.

Just before serving, blend egg yolks and cream. Add a small amount of the thickened sauce to the yolk mixture and mix well. Return to the thickened sauce with remaining tablespoon butter and stir with a wire whisk or fork until butter melts. Serve hot.

EGG SAUCE

6 hard boiled eggs
1 tablespoon fresh chopped parsley
¼ teaspoon dried tarragon
¼ teaspoon rosemary
1 teaspoon chives, or ½ teaspoon
  grated onion
1 clove garlic, mashed
2 teaspoons lemon juice
¼ teaspoon grated lemon rind
2 teaspoons dry mustard
¼ teaspoon paprika
1 teaspoon salt
4 tablespoons cream
4 tablespoons oil

1. Cut eggs in half. Separate yolks and whites. Chop the whites finely. Force the yolks through a strainer.

2. Add parsley, tarragon, rosemary, chives or onion and garlic. Mix well.

3. Add lemon juice and rind, mustard, paprika and salt. Mix well.

4. Stir in cream and oil. Refrigerate until ready to use.

ADDITIONAL ACCOMPANIMENTS
FOR BEEF FONDUE

Condiments:

Seasoned salt	Ground pepper
Hickory smoked salt	Ground ginger
Paprika	Onion powder

Sauces:

Hollandaise Sauce	Worcestershire Sauce
Bordelaise Sauce	Other meat sauces
Pepper Relish Mayonnaise	Mustard Mayonnaise
Anchovy Mayonnaise	Soy Sauce
Tomato Mayonnaise	Sweet and Sour Sauce

Relishes, Etcetera:

Hot and mild mustard	Pickled beets
Pickled onions	Peanuts

Olives (green or ripe)	Carrot curls
Capers	Dilled Cucumbers
Scallions	Mustard Pickles
Celery Fans	Gherkins
Radishes	Chutney

ORIENTALE FONDUE

This variation of Fondue Bourguignonne is adapted from the Chinese style of cooking; yet all equipment, cooking directions and quantities are the same. The only difference is substituting bouillon for the hot oil.

In this variation you've eliminated the possibility of smoking oil as well as the onus of fried foods. You're left with a tasty meat morsel cooked in bubbling bouillon.

You only need to maintain a pot of simmering bouillon at the ready on the kitchen stove to replenish the liquid in the fondue pot.

At the party's end save all the leftover bouillon. Next day, add some cooked mixed vegetables, a chopped tomato and a small amount of cooked rice. Warm, allowing one teaspoon sherry for each cup, and you have a delicious vegetable soup, its flavor enhanced by your meat cooking party.

SHRIMP FONDUE

Now heed this, waist-watchers and special dieters!

Shrimp fondue was devised so you could join in the fondue fun. It's the same as Orientale. Pots, plates, forks, sauces, cooking and serving directions — all are the same.

Added calories and fried foods are elimi_ nated when you cook the shrimp in boiling chicken consommé.

Enjoy, enjoy, enjoy!

Allow two pounds raw shrimp (average size) for four persons. Fresh or frozen is fine. But you decide who shells and deveins them. Check the fish store as there's quite a variance in price.

To cook, just spear the shrimp on a fork and cook in the consommé until they turn a party pink. No more than four or five minutes or they will be tough and rubbery.

TYPICAL SHELLFISH FONDUE MENU

SHRIMP FONDUE

TARTAR SAUCE   LEMON BUTTER

CUCUMBER SAUCE

CHIVE BUTTER   CAPER SAUCE

SOY SAUCE

STEAMED RICE   TOSSED SALAD

COFFEE OR TEA

CHERRY OR APPLE PIE

SEAFOOD SAUCES

Cucumber Sauce:

1 medium cucumber
½ cup sour cream
¼ cup mayonnaise
1 tablespoon grated onion
1 tablespoon minced parsley
2 teaspoons lemon juice

1. Scoop the seeds out of the unpeeled cucumber. Grate and drain.

2. Mix with the remaining ingredients.

3. Season to taste.

4. Chill.

Caper Sauce:

1 cup mayonnaise
3 tablespoons drained, chopped capers
2 teaspoons chopped parsley
1 teaspoon lemon juice
1½ teaspoons mustard

1. Mix all ingredients.

2. Chill for at least one hour before serving.

RAREBITS AND RABBITS

No one is sure how to spell or pronounce this word.

Some say a Welsh chieftain had unexpected company for dinner and no game to serve. He melted cheese, poured it over hot toast and tongue-in-cheek, called it Welsh Rabbit!

Others claim it's rarebit — a rare bit of good food.

Rarebit or rabbit, it is basically a fondue made with Cheddar cheese and beer, and

poured over toast. No matter which of the many variations we make, today we call it rabbit.

TYPICAL BRUNCH MENU

CHILLED VEGETABLE JUICE COCKTAILS

WELSH RABBIT

GRILLED SAUSAGE AND HAM

VINAIGRETTE COLE SLAW

COFFEE   TEA   COCOA

MELON BALLS

BROWNIES

CLASSIC WELSH RABBIT

1 egg
⅔ cup beer
2 tablespoons butter
3 cups grated sharp Cheddar cheese
1 teaspoon Worcestershire
¼ teaspoon dry mustard
Dash of cayenne
4 slices hot toast

1. Beat egg and beer together.

2. Melt butter and cheese in double boiler until thick.

3. Add seasonings.

4. Add beer and egg mixture to cheese. Heat, stirring constantly to prevent curdling or a skin forming on top.

5. Pour over hot toast.

Serves 4.

VARIATIONS OF BASIC WELSH RABBIT

ANCHOVY RABBIT

Omit the salt. Add 2 tablespoons anchovy paste. Put several anchovy fillets on top of rabbit mixture and grill until golden brown.

SARDINE RABBIT

Add ¼ cup tomato paste and a pinch of basil. Put boned sardines on top of basic rabbit and grill.

BACON RABBIT

Crumble crisp bacon on the top just before serving, *or,* sauté a slice of Canadian

53

bacon and place on hot toast before pouring on the rabbit. Sprinkle with paprika.

GOLDEN BUCK

Top each serving with a poached egg.

PARMESAN RABBIT

3 tablespoons butter
1 cup grated Parmesan cheese
4 eggs, lightly beaten
Salt and pepper to taste

1. Melt cheese and butter together.

2. Add small amount of hot cheese mixture to the beaten eggs. Mix well. Return to the pot with rest of cheese stirring constantly until smooth.

3. Add salt and pepper to taste.

4. Pour over hot toast fingers.

Serves 4.

DESSERT FONDUES

An American restaurateur is said to have invented Chocolate Fondue. This is a fitting tribute as chocolate was unknown in Europe before America's discovery.

Very rich and very good, it's excellent for a late evening snack in place of the usual coffee and cake.

Special pottery bowls can be purchased with a wrought iron stand and candle warmer. These are ideal as too high a flame will scorch the chocolate. For a large group use your chafing dish.

The chocolate sauce stays thin enough to be used for dunking quite a while after it is removed from the heat. So give each guest a demi-tasse cup filled with hot chocolate fondue set on a snack plate and surrounded with dunkables, if you prefer.

DUNKABLES

Dunkables can be anything that goes well with chocolate.

Think of all the outstanding chocolate candies you've eaten through the years, and no doubt you will be able to dream up some delicious variations of your very own!

Here are some suggestions to get you started:

Lady fingers, cut into chunks.

Angel food or pound cake, cut into ¾"
squares. (After cutting let stand open to
the air or toast the pound cake slightly.
This will harden the cakes slightly and
prevent their slipping off the fork into the
thick chocolate sauce.)

Marshmallows.

Popcorn.

Small caramels.

OTHER DUNKABLES

Fresh fruits:

Apple slices

Orange sections

Tangerine sections

Strawberries

Seedless grapes

Pineapple chunks

Peach slices

Bananas

Melon balls, marinated
  in lemon juice

Pour boiling water over the hulled strawberries to intensify the red color.

Canned fruit, well drained in paper towels:

Mandarin oranges

Fruit salad

Pineapple chunks

Apricots

Pear halves

Maraschino cherries,
  red and green

Insert a toothpick in *each* piece of fruit. Place in a single layer on a waxed paper-lined tray. Place in the freezer for about 2 hours. Remove about 10 minutes before serving to give the fruit a chance to defrost slightly. Dip the frosty fruit in the chocolate sauce and hold over the cup a few moments until the chocolate hardens.

MOCHA FONDUE

2 to 3 small Swiss chocolate bars (3 oz. each)
2 to 3 tablespoons cream
½ teaspoon powdered instant coffee
Pinch of cinnamon

1. Melt chocolate with cream over low heat, stirring constantly.

2. Add instant coffee and stir until well blended.

Serves 4.

Note: Instead of the instant coffee, substitute a coffee liqueur.

FONDUE À L'ORANGE

2 (4-ounce) milk chocolate bars
½ cup heavy cream
4 strips orange rind

1. Melt chocolate with cream over low heat, stirring constantly.

2. Add orange rind.

Note: The longer this fondue stands, the stronger the orange flavor, due to the oil in the rind permeating the chocolate. Try to make it the night before.

Variation:

Use orange liqueur in place of strips of orange rind.

THIS VOLUME
HAS BEEN PREPARED
PRINTED AND PUBLISHED
AT THE OFFICE OF
THE PETER PAUPER PRESS
MOUNT VERNON
NEW YORK